Susan Gibbons-Wolf is a freelance writer and author of the award-winning picture book *P.S. Boats, Around Puget Sound*. She studied creative writing at the University of Washington and is a trained public information officer. Teaching children for more than 40 years and working in public service has given her perspective of what children want: vivid illustrations, engaging text, heartfelt messages, and worthy subjects. She is the mother of three, grandmother of four, and lives with her husband on the beautiful Olympic Peninsula in Washington State, USA.

The Pirates' CODE

Susan Gibbons-Wolf

Austin Macauley Publishers™
London • Cambridge • New York • Sharjah

Copyright © Susan Gibbons-Wolf 2024

All rights reserved. No part of this publication may be reproduced, distributed, or transmitted in any form or by any means, including photocopying, recording, or other electronic or mechanical methods, without the prior written permission of the publisher, except in the case of brief quotations embodied in critical reviews and certain other non-commercial uses permitted by copyright law. For permission requests, write to the publisher.

Any person who commits any unauthorized act in relation to this publication may be liable to criminal prosecution and civil claims for damages.

Ordering Information
Quantity sales: Special discounts are available on quantity purchases by corporations, associations, and others. For details, contact the publisher at the address below.

Publisher's Cataloging-in-Publication data
Gibbons-Wolf, Susan
The Pirates' Code

ISBN 9798886935813 (Paperback)
ISBN 9798886935820 (ePub e-book)

Library of Congress Control Number: 2024906452

www.austinmacauley.com/us

First Published 2024
Austin Macauley Publishers LLC
40 Wall Street, 33rd Floor, Suite 3302
New York, NY 10005
USA

mail-usa@austinmacauley.com
+1 (646) 5125767

Dedicated to my sweetheart and husband, Jan Peter Wolf, who continues to surprise and delight me, and to the amazing people at Austin Macauley Publishers who believed my words could become a best-selling book. I also write in memory of Ryan Belknap Krug whose story of standing up for his friends inspired this book.

First, to the people of Austin Macauley who granted me my first publishing contract, thank you! To the people at Kidpower International who train educators and parents to help children be safe and confident in a challenging world, your work inspires us all. To the tireless public school teachers of our country, including my mother, who work so hard, oftentimes in deteriorating facilities with a shortage of materials, difficult children, and parents who occasionally don't understand – all our gratitude. To organizations like the YMCA, Boys and Girls Clubs, DOVE, and others that strive to improve the lives of parents and children, your work was never more needed than now. More information and resources about bullying prevention and pirates are found at the back of this book.

Chapter 1
Changes

Davy's mother walked him to his new elementary school.

"Class, this is Davy Stanton," his teacher said. "He's new, so let's welcome him with our best smiles and let him join in our activities." She pointed out a desk for him, but when Davy sat down, the boy next to him whispered, "Those are stupid shoes." At recess, Davy ran out the door to the playground where several boys stood talking.

"Hey, new kid, where'd you get that shirt?" Davy turned to see who was talking to him. It was a boy he recognized from class named Martin. "Nobody wears that kind of shirt here."

"My mom got me this shirt, and it's new," Davy said. "It's not nice to make fun of other people's clothes."

"Did your mommy teach you that, too?" asked another boy, and the group laughed. They ran off, and Davy tried hard not to cry. A girl with glasses standing nearby noticed them.

"Don't mind them," Ruby said, "they're always making fun of somebody."

Davy noticed a boy bouncing a ball against the side of the school. Although he spun his wheelchair around after it, it rolled out of reach. Davy ran over and got the ball.

"I'll play catch with you!" Davy offered.

"That would be awesome! My name's Jim."

"Hi, I'm Davy," he said with a big smile.

Back in class after recess, their teacher asked the children to quiet down.

"Now class," she said, "we have been working on spelling words. Davy, can you spell *animal*?"

"A-N-I-M…" said Davy with his southern accent. One of the girls nearby snickered.

"He talks funny." Davy stopped. Some children laughed. "Class, Davy was talking. Students need to listen and take turns," their teacher said, frowning. Davy continued but he had to blink back tears.

Chapter 2
The Problem

"What's wrong, Davy?" his mother asked when he got home from school.

"Kids at school," he gasped, trying not to cry, "were mean . . . to me today. They made fun of my clothes . . . and said I talk funny."

"We *are* new here," his mother said thoughtfully. "Your dad's family moved a lot when he was growing up because his daddy was in the military. Your dad was often the new kid in class. Why not ask him if he has some ideas for making friends?" Davy went to his dad who was in the garage.

"Dad, the kids at my school are mean. Mom said you moved a lot when you were young and know about being the new kid in class. What did you do?" Davy's dad put his wrench down and stepped away from the car.

"What happened?" he asked.

"Kids made fun of my clothes, and a girl said I talk funny." Davy started to cry. His dad hugged him.

"That must have hurt. Sometimes it's helpful to remember that most kids were new at some time. I don't know if this would work for you, but one time I found a friend, and we made a pirates' code of honor."

Chapter 3
The Code

"Pirates' code?" Davy wiped the tears on his cheeks and looked up, wide-eyed.

"Yes! You see, Davy, most kids want to belong, so if one kid makes fun of someone, then others join in. That way they feel they belong with their friends, but it doesn't make them happy. I started my own group of friends, and we made up a code." Davy sat close to his dad.

"What was your code like?" His dad rubbed his chin.

"It was a long time ago; let's see if I remember.

THE PIRATES' CODE OF HONOR

P - Stands for please come aboard, matey!
I - is for I can talk pirate.
R - means reach out in friendship.
A - stands for adventures are fun!
T - means tell it like it is.
E - is for explore new ideas. And
S means stand up for each other with smiles.
P-I-R-A-T-E-S, Pirates!"

"That's cool! Tell me more, Dad," Davy said, jumping up and hopping around. His dad began explaining the code.

"Please, come aboard. This means we welcome others to join us. As long as they follow the Pirates' Code, we will have fun together.

I can talk pirate. It's fun to have a special language we can share. Learning new words is good for our brain.

Reach out in friendship. We invite others to join us in having fun with kindness, respect, and safety.

Adventures are fun! We learn about our world and have fun.

Tell it like it is. Our words are honest and kind. We are brave enough to speak the truth.

Explore new ideas. We can learn how to do things like using a compass or following a map.

Stand up for each other with smiles. We stick together with respect. This means if one of us is being bullied, others come to his aid and stand by him. We grin big, no matter what our teeth look like, because smiles make friends."

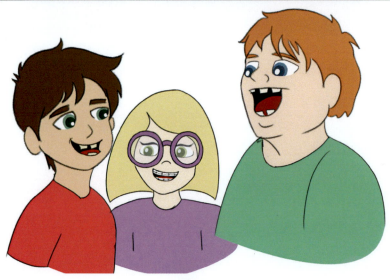

Chapter 4
The Enemy

While Davy was talking with his parents, his classmate Martin came home to an empty house. His mother was still at work.

"I'm hungry," said Henry, Martin's little brother.

"Shut up, baby," Martin said. "You know there's nothing until mom fixes us dinner."

"But my tummy hurts, Martin!"

"What do you want me to do about it?" Martin felt irritated because he was hungry too, but they didn't have much food. All they had were things like dried beans, which Martin didn't know how to cook. That made him scared, and when he was scared, he felt mad.

The next morning, Martin was wakened by his mother.

"I have to go to work early today, Martin. You'll have to wake up Henry and get him ready for school. I'll see you when I get home." She kissed Martin goodbye.

"Why do I always have to take care of Henry, Mom?"

"You're a great big brother, Martin. I wish things were different, but I have to work. See you later son."

Martin was still grouchy and yelled, "C'mon, Henry, wake up and get dressed!"

"Oh, do I have to?" Henry replied sleepily.

"Get up *now*, baby," Martin said crossly. He sure didn't like being in charge of Henry. When they went to school, Martin saw Jim trying to bounce a ball from his wheelchair. Martin grabbed it and kicked it against the brick wall of the school. It felt good to get his anger out, but when the ball hit the wall, instead of bouncing, it let out a little whine and went flat.

Martin laughed, "Stupid school! They can't even give us good play stuff."

Davy heard Martin. He thought about what Martin had said and saw how angry he was much of the time. When they went back to the classroom, Davy was still thinking about the ball. Just the day before, some older girls had been complaining that their volleyball net had holes in it.

Chapter 5
The Idea

That Thursday, Davy had an idea. He began making invitations to a pirates' meeting. He drew a skull and crossbones on a black flag and wrote:

"Aye-aye, matey! Blast ye if ye dinna come to me meeting. Come to the landlubber ship at 2215 Maple Avenue at 3:30 p.m. after school next Tuesday. Ye'll have a feast."

Davy made black eye patches and mustaches out of art foam. He went to a Dollar store and found bandanas.

"Mom," asked Davy, "can you make cookies? Please, please, please!" His mother laughed.

"Sure, Davy, but let's have some fruit and cheese, too."

"Aye, aye, captain." Davy grinned.

At school, Davy gave an invitation to Jim and Ruby. Then he gave an invitation to Cecil and one to Stan, his neighbor. On Tuesday, all the kids showed up at his house.

Ruby put on the mustache and began to giggle. Everyone laughed. "Take pictures!" Cecil said.

Davy's mom helped them make simple costumes out of old clothes. Then Davy explained the pirates' code, and they all agreed to follow it. They practiced talking like pirates and ate cookies. Davy's mom suggested they have a pirate movie night.

Chapter 6
Pirates Unite!

On Wednesday at school, a kid made fun of Jim for not being able to run with the basketball. Cecil stood beside Jim and said, "He can toss a ball to me."

When a girl called Ruby "four-eyes," Davy said, "Hey, please don't call her names. She's my friend." Stan stood beside Davy.

"She's my friend, too." The playground teacher noticed them.

"Davy, I'm giving you and your friends a 'Gotcha' Award because I caught you being kind," she said.

"It's all part of our pirates' code!" Davy said.

The next week, Jim's mother invited the group to her house where they made little boats.

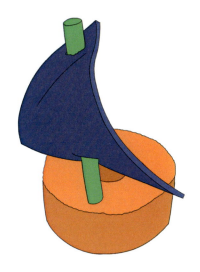

Cecil's mom took everyone to a naval museum so they could see the history of boats and submarines. Stan's dad taught the pirates how to use a compass. Ruby's dad invited the children and their parents to a beginning kayaking class.

Chapter 7
A Carnival

The next week at school, their teacher made an announcement.

"Class, the PTA is having a carnival in a few weeks to raise money for some new playground and sports equipment. They need ideas and help with booths for kids to play games, have their faces painted, and so on. You kids are smart, and I'll bet you can figure out some ways to help us out. Be sure to ask your parents to participate as well."

When Davy got home, he sat down at the kitchen table. He thought the Pirates could do face painting or disguises with the help of their parents.

Then Davy's mother, who was reading a history book, said, "Davy, here's a quote I find interesting. 'Emperor Sigismund was criticized for being kind to his enemies instead of destroying them. "What?" said the noble monarch. "Do I not destroy my enemies when I make them my friends?" Later, it was said that President Abraham Lincoln said that same thing and appointed some of his campaign rivals to his administration."

Davy thought about this. But how could he make friends with Martin and his buddies? He decided to ask the Pirates at their next meeting when they were talking about the carnival.

"I know," said Ruby. "We could have a skit! Those boys like to fight, so maybe we could have a make-believe sword fight."

"And walking the plank, but there's a shark!" Jim added.

Another pirate said, "But one of the bad guys becomes good by saving the doomed sailor from the shark!"

"We'd have to practice after school." Davy said. "I'd like to invite the bullies. They want good sports equipment too."

Chapter 8
The Solution

The next day, Davy asked the playground monitor to come with him and Jim to talk to Martin and his friends.

"Hey, we didn't do anything!" Martin said.

"Oh, you're not in trouble," the teacher said. "Davy has an idea for the carnival he'd like to tell you about."

After explaining his idea, Davy went on, "We'd have to have practices after school, and my mom always makes us cookies and snacks." That got Martin's attention.

"Can my little brother come too?" Martin asked hesitantly.

"Sure," Davy said eagerly. "The more, the merrier!"

"I'll ask my mom," Martin said. He smiled at Davy.

On Wednesday, Martin came up to Davy and said, "My mom said it was okay, and she called your mom to make sure."

"That's great!" Davy said. Pretty soon the children were meeting after school several times a week. They practiced faking a fall overboard and making their sword fights look real without hurting one another. They practiced talking like pirates. They made tickets to sell at the carnival to raise money for sports equipment. Davy's father and some of the other dads helped with sets for their skit.

They laughed, ate snacks, and had fun.

Something surprising was happening: Everyone was planning together. Everyone was working together, and everyone was having fun together!

Chapter 9
The Skit

On the day of the carnival, the group put on their skit. Davy, Jim, Ruby, and a couple of others took their found gold to the ship.

Suddenly, Martin's friends attacked them.

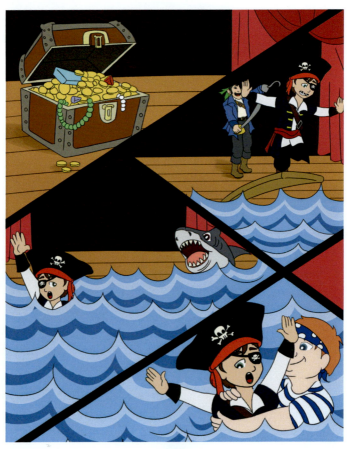

A sword fight broke out, but when Davy fell overboard, Martin yelled, "There's a shark! Let's save him!" Martin's friends all helped pull Davy out of the water.

"Oh, thanks, Martin!" Davy said. "Let's not fight anymore. How about we share the treasure equally?" All the pirates cheered. The audience applauded and whistled. The skit was a roaring success!

Chapter 10
The Results of Honor

In class after the carnival, Davy's teacher said, "I'm pleased to announce the carnival was a great success and you will soon see some new equipment coming to our school. I want to especially thank the Pirates for their skit, which everyone enjoyed. I have a little prize for each one of you for participating."

On the next parent-teacher day, Davy's teacher said to his mother, "I'm so glad Davy is in my class. Pirates stick together if one of them is being bullied. The kids who were struggling have found new friends and learned to work together. Some of the children that were having behavior problems have calmed down. The students in my class are a lot happier because each child has friends, and because of that, I believe more learning taking place."

When Davy's dad got home, he asked, "How's the pirates' code working out?"

"Oh, Dad," said Davy, "I have so many friends now! We stick up for each other. Those other kids have stopped making fun of us, and the kids who were acting mean are now my friends!"

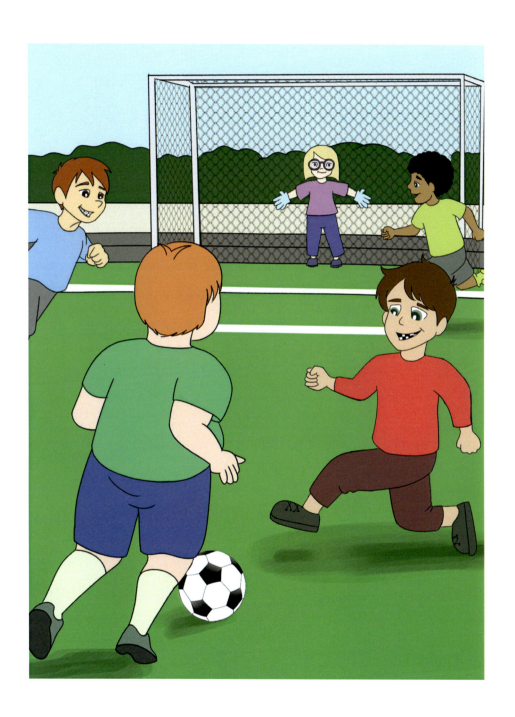

Resources for Parents and Educators

8 Skills for Preventing Bullying

Skill #1: Act with Awareness, Calm, Respect, and Confidence

People are less likely to bother you and more likely to listen to you if you walk, sit, and act with awareness, calm, respect, and confidence. Projecting a positive, assertive attitude means holding your head high, keeping your back straight, walking briskly, looking around, and having a peaceful face and body. Staying aware also helps you notice problems so you can deal with them sooner rather than later. Show young people the difference between being passive, aggressive, and assertive in body language, tone of voice, and choice of words.

Practice 1.1. Have your students walk across the floor, giving them directions on how to be successful by saying, "Walk with calm, respectful confidence toward (a location across the space)," and give positive, constructive feedback, such as: "Now take bigger steps," or "Look around you," or "Straighten your back," and "That's great!"

Skill #2: Leave in a Powerful, Positive Way

The best self-defense tactic is called 'target denial,' which means 'don't be there.' Leaving an unsafe situation is often the wisest and most effective solution for getting away from trouble.

Practice 2.1. Act out a scenario where a young person is walking in the school corridor (or any other place where they might be bullied). You can pretend to be a bigger kid who is acting aggressively by standing by the wall saying mean things. Ask first what these mean things might be because what is considered insulting or upsetting is different for different people, times, and places. If you can't think of what to say, just point your finger at the person practicing and yell, "BLAH! BLAH! BLAH!"

Practice 2.2. Coach each student to veer around you when you are pretending to bully, in order to move out of your reach. Remind students to leave with awareness, calm, and respectful confidence, glancing back to see where the person who is bullying is. Coach your student to leave in an assertive way, saying something neutral in a normal tone of voice like, "See you later!" or "Have a nice day!" Point out that stepping out of line or changing seats is often the safest choice for getting away from someone who is acting unsafely.

Skill #3: Set Boundaries about Disrespectful or Unsafe Behavior

Remind children and teens that your values are to have a welcoming and safe environment for everyone and that being cruel or hurtful is wrong, whether it happens in person, via social media, by texting, online, or in any other way. Set a good example by being thoughtful about what you say and do. Address immediately any prejudiced language or remarks, even if it is 'just a joke.' Teach young people how to speak up about disrespectful language directed at themselves or others by saying, "That didn't sound kind," or, "That sounds prejudiced," or, "Please stop saying that." Be clear that you will understand if they don't feel safe speaking up and that then their job is to get adult help.

Boundaries can also be important in dealing with aggressive or threatening behavior in situations where it is not possible to just leave. Waiting and wishing for a safety problem to go away on its own usually just gives time for the problem to get bigger. Of course, if this is happening, you are going to take action to stop this behavior right away. However, if your student is worried or has had this problem in the past, practicing how to get away safely in the moment can be very empowering. Ask the student for examples, such as being followed or trapped in the bathroom or hallway.

Practice 3.1. Pretend to follow each student and then very gently pretend to poke them in the back. Do this very carefully; the purpose is to practice what to do rather than be hurtful or scary. Coach your student to turn, stand up tall, put hands up in front of his or her body like a fence, elbows bent to be close to the body, palms out and open, and say loudly, "Stop!" Move back and coach your student to walk away.

Practice 3.2. Now pretend to be blocking the door in a classroom or bathroom. Point your finger at your student and yell, "BLAH! BLAH! BLAH!" Coach your student to set boundaries using a calm but clear voice and polite, firm words – not whiny and not aggressive. For example, say, "STOP! Please get out of my way. I just want to leave. Get out of my way. I just want to go!" Step aside and coach your student to walk away.

Children and teens need support to learn and use these skills. Encourage them for trying even if they don't get it right to begin with. Realize this might be very hard and triggering for young people (and maybe for you too).

Skill #4: Use Your Voice
Most young people who are being hurtful to others on purpose don't want to get caught. Yelling and speaking up loudly calls attention to a bullying problem or any kind of unsafe behavior. Suppose they are being threatened physically or dealing with another kid who pushes, shoves, trips, or hits. You can practice by pretending you are about to act unsafely without actually doing anything hurtful.

Practice 4.1. Coach students to pull away and yell "NO! STOP! LEAVE! HELP!" really loudly. Coach them to yell, "STOP! I don't like that!" Coach them to make their body tall, look the person who is bullying in the eye, and speak in a firm voice with both hands in front of their body, palms facing outward, like a wall.

Practice 4.2. If this doesn't work right away, practice how to yell for help in a way that will call attention to the problem. For example, "STOP! GET OUT OF MY WAY! HELP! GET THE TEACHER! _____ (name) IS BULLYING ME!" Remind students to leave and go to an adult to report what happened and get help as soon as possible.

Skill #5: Protect Your Feelings from Name-Calling and Hurtful Behavior
Most schools, youth groups, and families want to provide a caring environment. The reality is, no matter how committed we are to safety and respect, not all places have the same commitment – and even when they do, people will still make mistakes. For this

reason, learning how to protect their feelings from insults can prepare children and teens to take charge of their emotional safety all their lives. Discuss with students how saying, writing, emailing, or texting in ways that are hurtful to anyone makes problems bigger, not better. Their job is to stay in charge of what they say and do, no matter how they feel inside.

The Kidpower Trashcan Technique helps take the power out of hurting words by hearing them said aloud, catching them, and imagining throwing them away. Doing this physically and out loud will help students avoid taking in hurtful words in their imagination.

Practice 5.1. Catch and throw the mean things that other people are saying into a trashcan. Coach students to then use positive self-talk to say something positive out loud to themselves to take in. For example, if someone says, "I don't like you," you can throw those words away and say, "I like myself." If someone says, "You are stupid," you can throw those words away and say, "I'm smart." If someone says, "I don't want to play with you," then you can throw those words away and say, "I will find another friend."

For additional ways to protect your feelings at any age, see, 'triggers, emotional attacks, and emotional safety techniques' on Kidpower's website.

Skill #6: Speak up for Positive Inclusion

Being left out for reasons that have nothing to do with behavior is a major form of bullying. Exclusion of this kind should be clearly against the rules at school, in recreational activities, and in all youth groups. That said, it is important to realize that sometimes kids (and adults) avoid someone because of their hurtful or negative behavior. In that case, adult leadership is essential in helping that young person develop more positive social skills and negotiate win-win relationships.

In addition to getting adult help, a child or teen who is being excluded can practice asking to join a game in a respectful, persistent, and powerful way.

Practice 6.1. Start by pretending to be a kid who is playing a game with a group and wants to leave someone out. Coach each student to walk up and say cheerfully and firmly, "I want to play."

Practice 6.2. Coach your student to sound and look confident and friendly, not whiny or aggressive. Ask your students for the reasons kids give for excluding others. Use those reasons so your students can practice persisting. For example, if the reason is, "You're not good enough," your students can practice saying, "I'll get better if I practice!" If the reason is, "There are too many already," your students might practice saying, "There's always room for one more." If the reason is, "You cheated last time," your students might practice saying, "I did not understand the rules. Let's make sure we agree on the rules this time."

See Kidpower's article: "Shunning & Exclusion: Kidpower Skills for Protecting Children from Relational Bullying."

Skill #7: Be Persistent in Getting Help from Busy Adults

Children and teens who are being bullied need to be able to tell teachers, parents, and other adults in charge what is happening in the moment clearly and calmly and persistently, even if these adults are very distracted or rude and even if asking for help has not worked before. Explain that telling to get help is not the same as tattling to just to get someone in trouble. Learning how to have respectful, firm words, body language, and tone of voice even under pressure and not giving up when asking for help are lifelong skills.

We have found that rehearsing what to say and do is helpful for both children and adults in learning how to persist and get help when you need it.

Practice 7.1. Pretend to be a teacher, coach, or someone else who kids might expect help and support from. Tell your students who you are pretending to be and where you might be. Coach your students to start saying in a clear, calm voice, "Excuse me, I have a safety problem."

Now, pretend to be busy and just ignore the student practicing. Coach them to keep going and to say, "Excuse me, I really need your help."

Act irritated and impatient and say, "Yes. What is it now?" and keep acting busy.

Coach your student to explain the problem objectively without using insults in a calm and strong voice. For example:

- "We have a safety problem. The kids over there are calling me names and not letting me play the game. I told them I don't like being called names and that I want to play, but they won't listen."
  Or:
- "Those boys keep coming up and pushing me. I tried to stay away from them, but they keep coming up to me and won't leave me alone."

Even though we want children and teens to learn to solve their problems themselves, we also want them to get help when they are not yet able to handle a problem on their own. They need to realize their adults might not have noticed what happened even if we were standing right there.

To give practice in persisting, coach your students to deal with a variety of common adult reactions, such as saying, "That's nice!" as if you heard but did not actually listen. Or make irritated, minimizing, or blaming comments such as, "I'm busy!" or "Solve it yourself!" or "What's the big deal? Just stay away from those kids!" or even worse, "Don't be a tattletale."

Practice 7.2. Coach your students to persist in getting help by throwing away the hurting words the difficult adult you are pretending to be said to them. Have them do this by:

(1). Saying inside to themselves, "I have the right to get help."

(2). Touching your arm to get your attention

(3). Saying again, "Please, listen to me. This is important." Tell your students that sometimes adults don't understand. Instead of giving up, they can ask again and state the problem more strongly.

- "I do not feel safe here because (state specific problem again)."
  Or,
- "Having this happen is making me feel bad about going to school. Please, I really need you to listen." Or,
- "My parents told me I have the right to feel safe here, and it is your job to help me."

Now change your demeanor so your student can see you are listening and understanding. Say, "Oh! I am sorry I got irritated with you, and I am glad you are telling me. Tell me more, and we will figure out what to do."

Young people need to know that. Even if the adult in charge does not listen or is blaming, having someone harming them is not their fault. Their job is to keep asking the adults until someone does something to fix the problem. Tell the young people in your life to please always tell you whenever they have a safety problem with anyone, anywhere, anytime. Remember it is the responsibility of adults to create safe environments for the children and teens in their care and to be good role models by intervening to stop unsafe behavior and by acting as their advocates in powerful, respectful ways.

Skill #8: Use Physical Self-Defense as the Last Resort
Children and teens need to know when they have the right to hurt someone to stop that person from hurting them. At Kidpower, we teach that fighting is the last resort – when you are about to be harmed and you cannot leave or get help. Before we teach people of any age how to fight, we first make sure they have been successful in practicing how to take action that will prevent and avoid most physical fights.
Bullying problems are often not as clear cut as other personal safety issues. Families have different rules about where they draw the line. Also, many schools will suspend all students involved in a fight, so parents have to be prepared for this consequence.
Learning physical self-defense helps most children become more confident, even if they never have to use these skills in a real-life situation. Just being more confident helps children avoid being chosen as a victim most of the time. There are different self-defense techniques for bullying than for more dangerous situations. See Kidpower's article: *'How to Choose a Good Self-Defense Program.'*

The above is adapted and reprinted with permission from Kidpower. Read more about bullying and other skills for kids at www.kidpower.org. Its website states:

As a global nonprofit leader, Kidpower Teenpower Fullpower International is dedicated to providing empowering and effective child protection, positive communication, and personal safety strategies and skills to people of all ages and abilities all over the world. Our goal is that these 'people-safety' skills will help people to lead safer, more joyful lives and to create cultures of respect and safety for everyone, everywhere – and use of our program in different places by different people helps to further that goal.

Other Online Resources Dealing with Bullying

US Department of Health and Human Services, Prevention: Learn How to Identify Bullying and Stand up to It Safely, *www.stopbullying.gov*

www.stompoutbullying.org

Pirate Resources

Learn to talk like a pirate. Celebrate International Talk Like a Pirate Day. Learn pirate songs and more at http://talklikeapirate.com/wordpress/junior-pirates.

Make paper boats and hats. See YouTube instructions for a boat: https://www.youtube.com/watch?v=b3QZpBL8-Tg.
And for a paper hat:
 https://www.youtube.com/watch?v=OCJvzSuVT6Q.
For a larger hat that uses newspaper, see:
https://www.youtube.com/watch?v=E0oGg7It0BM.

Learn about orienteering(how to use a map and compass) at: https://boyslife.org/outdoors/outdoorarticles/3877/compass-tips-and-tricks/.

Those who fight bad pirates are the U.S. Navy and the U.S. Coast Guard.

Naval Museums

Hampton Roads Naval Museum – Norfolk, VA

National Museum of the American Sailor (formerly Great Lakes Naval Museum) – Great Lakes, IL

National Naval Aviation Museum – Pensacola, FL

Naval Undersea Museum – Keyport, WA

Naval War College Museum – Newport, RI

Puget Sound Navy Museum – Bremerton, WA

Submarine Force Museum & Historic Ship Nautilus – Groton, CT

U.S. Naval Academy Museum – Annapolis, MD

U.S. Navy Seabee Museum – Port Hueneme, CA and North Kingstown, RI

U.S. Navy Memorial Museum – Washington, DC

THE END